MAY 0 5 2005

Around The World With

FOOD AND SPICES

Salt

Melinda Lilly

Rourke Publishing LLC
Vero Beach, Florida 32964

For Chuck Reasoner, salt of the earth

PHOTO CREDITS:

Cover photo by Jayne McKay
Photo on title page: Detail of Salt Stacks. Photo courtesy of Cargill.
Page 7 Detail of a photo by Jean-Claude Latombe
Page 8 Photo by Scott M. Thompson. Salt shakers courtesy of Jayne McKay
Page 11 Salt Crystallizers. Photo courtesy of Cargill.
Page 12 Detail of La Generosite de Scipio, by Jean Charles Perrin. Photo courtesy of Sotheby's Picture Library, London.
Page 15 Detail of a photo by Jean-Claude Latombe
Page 16 Whistle, in the Form of a Warrior. Mayan, Island of Jaina, ca. 650 A.D. The Saint Louis Art Museum Credit Line
Page 19 Les Contenances de la Table, title page. [Lyons: Printer of the Champion des Dames (Jean De Pré)]. The Pierpont Morgan Library, New York. PML 63681.
Page 20 Frontispiece. Il Milione. Marco Polo. Photo by Scott M. Thompson
Page 23 Statue of Saint Barbara by Jozef Markowski. Photo by A. Slodkowscy
Page 24 Detail of "Hernando Cortés and the Spanish Soldiers Confront the Indians." Courtesy of the Library of Congress.
Page 27 Detail of The Taking of the Bastille. © Archivo Iconografico, S.A./CORBIS
Page 28 AP/WIDE WORLD PHOTOS

ILLUSTRATIONS:

Artwork on world map and additional illustrations by Patti Rule
Artwork on cover by James Spence

EDITORIAL SERVICES:

Pamela Schroeder

Library of Congress Cataloging-in-Publication Data

Lilly, Melinda.
  Salt / Melinda Lilly.
    p. cm. — (Around the world with food and spices)
  Includes bibliographical references and index.
  ISBN 1-58952-048-3
   1. Salt—Juvenile literature. [1. Salt.] I. Title

TX407.S25 L55 2001
553.6'32—dc21

200101640

Printed in the USA

Table of Contents

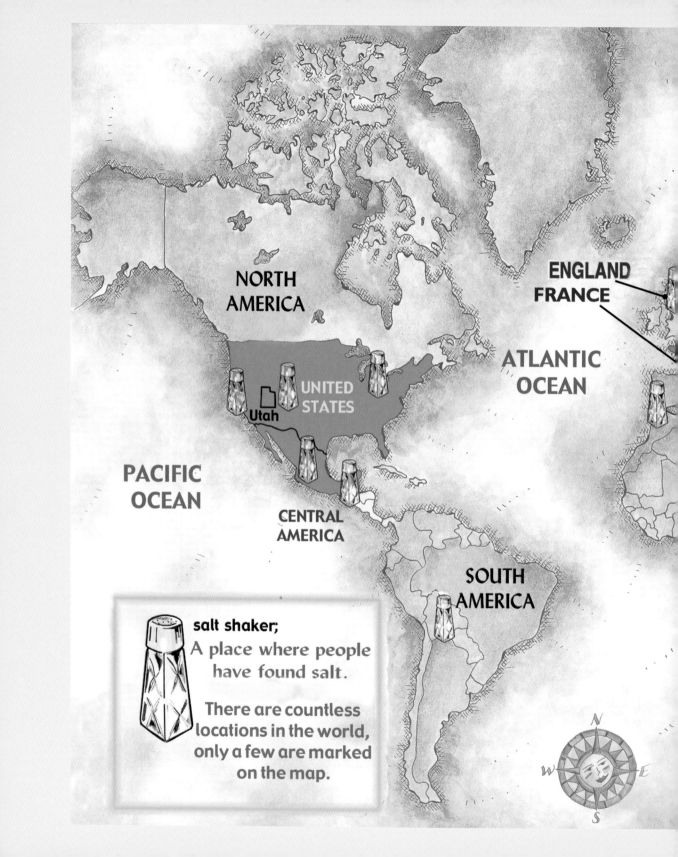

NORTH
AMERICA

ENGLAND
FRANCE

ATLANTIC
OCEAN

UNITED
STATES

Utah

PACIFIC
OCEAN

CENTRAL
AMERICA

SOUTH
AMERICA

salt shaker;
A place where people
have found salt.

There are countless
locations in the world,
only a few are marked
on the map.

N
W E
S

The salt shakers show some of the places where salt has been found.

Salt of the Earth

Can you answer this old riddle? Throw this rock into the water and it changes into water. What is it? Salt!

Dry salt is a rock. In water it **dissolves**, breaking apart until you can't see it.

Most salt comes from oceans, other salty water, and places where salt water has dried. If all the oceans' salt were piled on top of the United States, we would be covered in salt a mile high!

Blocks of salt in an African market

The Rock We Eat

In your body right now, you have about 3 ounces (85 grams) of salt. That is the same amount as 98 small salt packets given away at fast-food restaurants! We need salt to live. However, if we have too much, it is bad for our health.

When we cry, sweat, or go to the bathroom, we lose salt. We make up for what is lost by eating food with salt in it.

Salt shakers

Salt Town

Today salt is easy to find. Long ago it was often hard to locate salt lakes or rock salt that could be dug out of the earth. People even looked for spots where ocean water could **evaporate**, or turn into air, leaving only salt.

One of the oldest salt mines is below **Hallstatt**, Austria. The name *Hallstatt* means salt town. Salt has been mined there for almost 3,000 years.

This salt is being made from ocean water. Shrimp and colorful plants that live in the salt water turn it pink.

Salty Words

Long ago, people salted meat and fish to keep them from turning rotten. As a result, they needed lots of salt. They called it white gold because it cost as much as gold.

The ancient city of Rome, Italy, had its start as a place to buy and sell salt. Part of a Roman soldier's pay, or **salary**, was given to him in salt. Our word salary comes from the Roman word *salarium*, meaning salt money.

Roman soldiers were given salt as part of their pay.

Salt War

The Axum kingdom of Africa became rich by selling salt, gold, and gems. They built a palace and city in Ethiopia and protected their salt lakes. More than 1,500 years ago, people from a nearby tribe attacked an Axum camel train on its way to get salt. The Axum army took over all of the tribe's lands and put their king in jail.

Even in the 1900s, salt was still so important in Ethiopia that, instead of coins, money was bricks of salt.

Loading a camel with salt in Ethiopia

Mayan Salt

The ancient Maya of Central America made salt in drying ponds near the ocean. They also heated salt water in pots until the water was gone, or evaporated.

They used salt for many things besides eating. When a child was born, the parents tasted holy salt and sprinkled it inside their house. Soldiers' jackets were stuffed with salt to make them hard enough to stop arrows. They also offered salt to their gods as food.

This Mayan soldier whistle was made nearly 1,000 years ago. 17

With a Grain of Salt

    Have you ever tossed salt over your shoulder? People have been tossing salt over their shoulders since the early **Middle Ages**— more than 1,500 years ago! Why?

    In Europe, salt was holy. To spill it was bad luck. People believed that demons could sneak up behind a person who had spilled salt. Everyone knew that demons hated salt in their faces! People tossed salt over their shoulders to scare the demons away.

This picture showing demons is from a book about table manners printed in 1487.

Ɒⱬ
contenances de la table:

Salt at the End of the World

Joined by his father and uncle, Marco Polo traveled from Italy to the Kavir salt desert of Iran. Few had ever crossed it. Most Italians thought the Kavir was the end of the world.

Crossing the desert was hard. Salt broke under their feet, making it tough to walk. Water was too salty to drink. After about two weeks, the Polos reached the end of the desert.

Back in Italy in 1297, Marco Polo made a book about his journey to the Kavir and beyond.

This picture of Marco Polo is from the first printing of his book.

Worth Its Salt

In Poland there is a hidden world of treasure found 300 feet underground. There are statues of ghosts, holy men and women, and a church—all made of salt! For more than 700 years, people chipped at the greenish salt in this huge mine.

If you explored the 100 miles of tunnels, you would find underground lakes. One tall room has even been used for bungee jumping!

A Polish miner carved this statue of Saint Barbara out of salt. Miners believed Saint Barbara protected them as they worked.

War in Mexico

When Hernán Cortés and his Spanish soldiers came to Mexico in 1519, they soon made war. They attacked the Aztecs, a powerful people who controlled much of Mexico and its salt.

Cortés told other Mexican tribes that if they helped him fight the Aztecs he would give them salt and other things. They thought their lives would be better if they helped Cortés. However, after he won the war Cortés brought slavery and death to many in Mexico.

Spanish and Aztec soldiers

Salt and Freedom

For hundreds of years, most French people had to pay salt **tax**—extra money to the king every time they bought salt. This tax was famous for being unfair. Kings ordered some people to buy lots of salt and pay high taxes. Others paid no tax and could buy as little as they wanted.

The salt tax was one of the reasons people fought in the French Revolution in 1789. This war ended the rule of kings in France.

Soldiers fighting in the French Revolution

March to the Sea

The people of India were ruled by England, but they wanted to rule themselves. In 1930 Mahatma Gandhi, a famous Indian leader, led a march to the sea. His march was a **protest** against English rule.

After walking 240 miles, he gathered salt on the beach. It was against the law at that time to gather salt. England controlled all of India's salt and forced India's people to pay a salt tax. This protest and one held later at a salt factory helped India become free to rule itself.

Mahatma Gandhi leads the march to the sea.

Pour It On!

Today nearly every table has a salt shaker. Salt is no longer as costly as gold. It is so cheap people often give it away for free.

We still love salt, however. We use it in countless ways. Only five salt grains out of 100 are for food. People use salt to melt ice from roads. It is an ingredient in paints, glues, medicines, and more. It was even used in making the paper of this book!

Glossary

dissolves (dih ZOLVZ) — when something solid becomes part of a liquid

evaporate (ih VAP eh rate) — change from liquid into a gas, like water changing into steam

Hallstatt (HOLL stat) — a town in Austria and a Celtic word that means salt town

Middle Ages (MID ul AY jez) — European history from 476 to 1453

protest (PROH test) — to show that one is against an idea, action, or law

salary (SAL eh ree) — payment given in return for work

tax (TAKS) — a fee paid to a government by the people

Index

Further Reading

Hull, Robert. *The Aztecs.* Raintree Steck-Vaughn, 1998.
Leon, Vicki. *Wetlands: All About Bogs, Bayous, Swamps and a Salt Marsh or Two.* Silver Burdett Press, 1999.
Levchuck, Caroline M. *Kids During the Time of the Maya.* Power Kids Press, 1999.
Kenny Mann. *Egypt, Kush, Aksum: Northeast Africa.* Dillon Press, 1997.
Rachel Wright. *Paris, 1789 : A Guide to Paris on the Eve of the Revolution.* Kingfisher, 1999.

Websites to Visit

www.saltinstitute.org

About the Author

Melinda Lilly is the author of several children's books. Some of her past jobs have included editing children's books, teaching pre-school, and working as a reporter for *Time* magazine.